WF STUDIO

fashion design
WORKSHOP

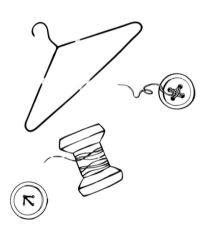

Walter Foster

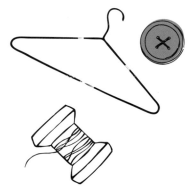

Associate Publisher: Elizabeth T. Gilbert
Project Manager: Rebecca J. Razo
Art Director: Shelley Baugh
Associate Editor: Emily Green
Production Artists: Debbie Aiken, Rae Siebels
Production Manager: Nicole Szawlowski
International Purchasing Coordinator: Lawrence Marquez

www.walterfoster.com
6 Orchard Road, Suite 100
Lake Forest, CA 92630

Printed in China
13 15 17 19 20 18 16 14 12

fashion design
WORKSHOP

By Stephanie Corfee

Table of Contents

Chapter 1:
Introduction to Fashion Design Drawing 7

Tools & Materials................................8

Drawing Techniques..........................10

Color Basics......................................11

Creating Texture...............................12

Fashion Terms...................................14

Figure Proportions............................16

Figure Poses.....................................18

Head & Face......................................20

Eyes & Lips.......................................21

Hairstyles...22

Arms & Hands...................................24

Legs & Feet......................................25

Using Mannequins............................26

Fashion Drawing Tips & Tricks..........27

Chapter 2:
Garments, Shoes & Accessories 29

Tops, Tees & Tanks...........................30

Jeans, Pants & Shorts.......................32

Skirts, Dresses & Gowns...................34

Sweaters, Jackets & Outerwear........36

Hats...38

Shoes & Handbags...........................40

Chapter 3:
Current Fashion Styles................................43

Chic & Trendy...................................44

Girly & Romantic..............................48

Fun & Casual....................................52

Confident & Classic..........................56

Athletic & Sporty..............................60

Bohemian & Eclectic.........................64

Rebellious & Daring..........................68

Skater Dude......................................72

Chapter 4:
Fabulous Fashions from History 77

'40s Swing..78

'50s Rock 'n' Roll..............................82

'60s Mod Squad................................86

'70s Disco...90

'80s New Wave..................................94

Chapter 5:
Custom Designs 99

Renaissance Era.............................100

Blushing Bride.................................104

Chapter 6:
Fashion Figure Templates 111

About the Artist...128

Chapter 1

Introduction to Fashion Design Drawing

Tools + Materials

The tools and materials on these pages will help you create all of the fabulous fashions in this book.

Sketchpad and Drawing Paper – Sketchpads come in many sizes and are great for working out your ideas.

Vellum Drawing Paper – Vellum is a heavyweight, smooth-finish cardstock that takes in color beautifully. It's perfect for finished drawings.

Tracing Paper – Tracing paper is useful for tracing figures and creating a clean version of a sketch using a light box. (See "How to Use a Light Box," page 9.) Use quality tracing paper that is sturdy enough to handle erasing and coloring.

Pencils – Graphite drawing pencils are designated by hardness and softness. H pencils are hard and make lighter marks; B pencils are soft and make darker marks. Pencils range from very soft (9B) to very hard (9H). For fashion drawing, I prefer mechanical pencils with .5mm lead. They are great for line quality and consistency of sharpness.

Kneaded Eraser – These moldable, stretchable erasers can be shaped into a fine point or used over broad surfaces. They leave no dust and are great for picking up excess color and lifting out highlights. They also work especially well at removing pencil marks from tracing paper.

White Plastic/Vinyl Eraser – Plastic or vinyl erasers are a staple in fashion drawing. They remove graphite without chewing up the paper and are best for erasing hard pencil marks and large areas.

Art Markers – Professional art markers create bold, vibrant bands of color. They are great for laying down large areas of even color, as well as for shading.

Colored Pencils – Colored pencils are a convenient and easy method for applying color. Professional-grade colored pencils have a waxy, soft lead that is excellent for shading and building up layers of color gradually.

Gel Pens – Gel pens consist of pigment suspended in a water-based gel. They deliver thick, opaque color and work easily on dark or previously colored surfaces. They are perfect for finishing details in your illustrations or for adding sparkles, stitching detail, and accents.

Pigment-Ink Pens – Technical pens are great for adding teeny, crisp details without bleeding.

How to Use a Light Box

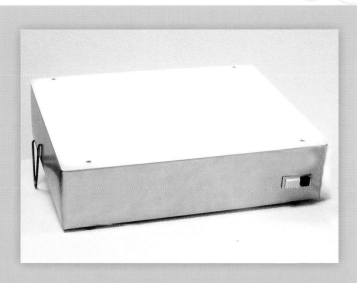

A light box is a useful and generally inexpensive tool (although there are fancier, professional-grade versions). As its name suggests, a light box is a compact box with a transparent top and light inside. The light illuminates papers placed on top, allowing dark lines to show through for easy tracing. Simply tape your rough drawing on the surface of the light box. Place a clean sheet of paper over your original sketch and turn the box on. The light illuminates the drawing underneath and will help you accurately trace the lines onto the new sheet of paper. You can also create a similar effect by placing a lamp under a glass table or taping your sketch and drawing paper to a clear glass window and using natural light.

Drawing Techniques

Warming Up

Warm up your hand by drawing random lines, scribbles, and squiggles. Familiarize yourself with the different lines that your pencils can create, and experiment with every stroke you can think of, using both a sharp point and a dull point.

Types of Strokes

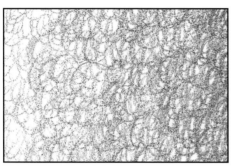

Circular Move your pencil in a circular motion, either randomly (shown here) or in patterned rows. For denser coverage, overlap the circles. Varying the pressure creates different textures.

Linear Move your pencil in the same direction, whether vertically, horizontally, or diagonally. Strokes can be short and choppy or long and even.

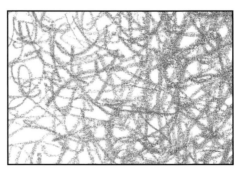

Scumbling Scribble your pencil in random strokes to create an organic mass. Changing the pressure and the amount of time you linger over the same area can increase or decrease the value of the color.

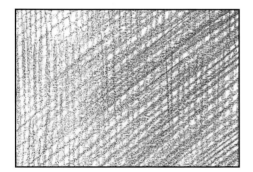

Hatching Sketch a series of roughly parallel lines. The closer the lines are to each other, the denser and darker the color. Crosshatching involves laying one set of hatched lines over another, but in a different direction.

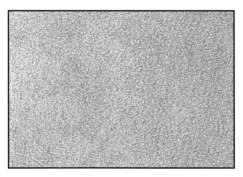

Smooth No matter what stroke you use, if you control the pencil, you can produce an even layer of color. You can also blend your strokes so that you can't tell how color was applied.

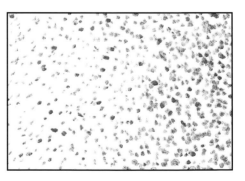

Stippling Sharpen your pencil and apply small dots all over the area. For denser coverage, apply the dots closer together.

Color Basics

Color means everything in fashion design, so it helps to know a bit about color theory. There are three *primary* colors: red, yellow, and blue. These colors cannot be created by mixing other colors. Mixing two primary colors produces a *secondary* color: orange, green, and purple. Mixing a primary color with a secondary color produces a *tertiary* color: red-orange, red-purple, yellow-orange, yellow-green, blue-green, and blue-purple. Red, orange, and yellow are "warm" colors, whereas green, blue, and purple are "cool" colors.

The Color Wheel

A color wheel is useful for understanding relationships between colors. Knowing where each color lies on the color wheel makes it easy to understand how colors relate to and react with one another. Colors directly across from one another, like yellow and purple, are *complementary*. Colors next to each other, like green and blue-green, are *analogous*.

Color Mixing

Color mixing is one of the most enjoyable parts of being a fashion designer. Use this handy guide to practice creating color combinations—then experiment creating your own!

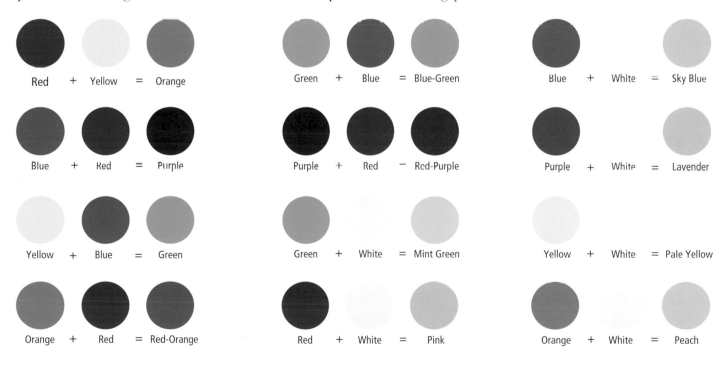

Red + Yellow = Orange

Green + Blue = Blue-Green

Blue + White = Sky Blue

Blue + Red = Purple

Purple + Red = Red-Purple

Purple + White = Lavender

Yellow + Blue = Green

Green + White = Mint Green

Yellow + White = Pale Yellow

Orange + Red = Red-Orange

Red + White = Pink

Orange + White = Peach

Creating Texture

Now that you're familiar with some basic pencil strokes and color theory, you can start practicing how to create an assortment of textures.

Plaid – Use marker for the base color. Add vertical and horizontal lines with colored pencil in groups of three, alternating between colors. In the example above, I used one red line inside two green lines for each grouping.

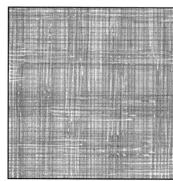

Tweed – Use marker for the base color, followed by crosshatching all over, alternating pencil colors. The key to this texture is adding lots of layers. Finish with a bit of white gel pen or a fine-tipped pigment ink pen to add definition.

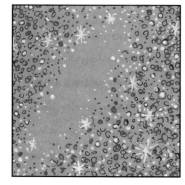

Sparkles/Sequins – Use marker for the base color. Then add lots of dots and circles using fine-tipped pigment ink pens and gel pens in black, white, and coordinating colors. Use a white gel pen to add stars and bursts for twinkle.

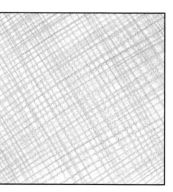

Netting/Tulle – Choose two or three analogous shades of colored pencil and create a diagonal crosshatched pattern. Keeping your pencils sharp will help create a more delicate-looking texture.

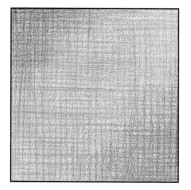

Denim – Start with a muted gray-green marker for the base color. Use colored pencils to add light crosshatching over the area in several different shades of blue and gray. Keep your pencil sharp so that you can still make out the crosshatching, which reads as a "woven" texture.

Shiny (patent leather, satin, etc.) – Creating a shiny texture is all about contrast. Lay down a bold color using marker, leaving some white areas of varying widths as you move across. Then add a few vertical stripes of a slightly darker shade.

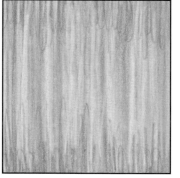

Layered Chiffon – Use a light-colored marker for the base. Gradually build up shading in a vertical pattern using analogous shades of colored pencil. Darken the areas around the gathers slightly, and finish with a white colored pencil to highlight the lightest areas in the folds.

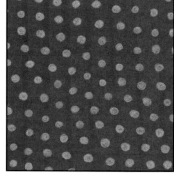

Polka Dots – Use marker for the base color. Then create an even pattern of circles with colored pencil. Use an index card or ruler to help keep the rows straight.

Lace – White lace can be indicated with light colors. Sketch a floral or paisley pattern. Then accent each shape with other light colors, such as cream, light yellow, and blue-gray colored pencils.

Appliqué – Use the same principles for creating a lace texture. Keep in mind that appliqués fill only a particular space—they are not all-over patterns.

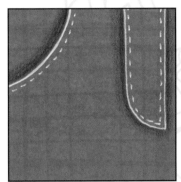

Topstitching – Use marker for the base color. Then draw the seam lines with pencil. Shade along the seams with a colored pencil in a shade or two darker than your background color. Finish by drawing solid and dotted lines right along the seam lines to indicate machine stitching.

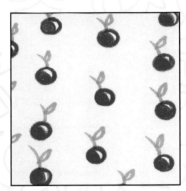

Print Fabric – Use marker for the base color. Then use colored pencil or marker to create a specific pattern, such as cherries or flowers. Use an index card or ruler to help keep the rows straight.

Gathered Hemline – Draw a wavy line where a straight hemline would be. To show the gathers, draw a short, straight vertical line from each wavy fold up into the garment, allowing the lines to fade off. Color the inside folds along the hemline a shade darker than the primary color of the fabric. Then, using a light hand, shade the vertical folds with a slightly darker, analogous pencil color.

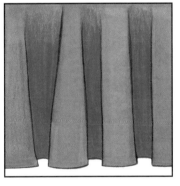

Pleated Hemline – To create a pleated hemline, draw a jagged horizontal line where a straight hemline would be. (Think of a straight line that has square "chunks" taken out.) To show the pleats, draw a short, straight vertical line from each corner of the jagged line up into the garment, allowing the lines to fade off. Using a light hand, shade the vertical recessed folds a shade darker than the primary color of the fabric.

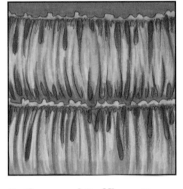

Gathers and Ruffles – Use marker for the base color. Draw ruffled "lettuce" edges horizontally; then draw a series of loops and curved lines to show where the fabric is gathered just below the edge. Shade the areas closest to the gathered edge in the darkest color, tapering out to lighter areas. Repeat this technique for each ruffled tier.

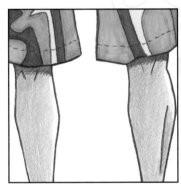

Hem Shading – A shadow will always be cast on the model's arm or leg at the point where a sleeve or pant leg ends. To capture this effect, draw a few hatch lines directly below the hem; then add a darker bit of colored pencil over the lines to show dimension. Hatch lines are similar to crosshatching strokes, but instead of drawing crisscrossed lines, you'll simply draw light parallel lines.

Fashion Terms

Below are some common terms in the fashion biz that you'll need to know if you're going to be the next hot runway designer!

Appliqué: A cut-out design that is sewn onto a garment as embellishment or decoration. Appliqués are decorated bits of fabric or cut-out bits of lace. They are often seen on wedding dresses or fancy evening gowns.

Bodice: The top of a garment that covers from the neck to the waist or hip.

Boning: Stiff strips made from polypropylene or spiral steel, which are sewn into vertical seams of a corset or dress bodice to help with shaping, structure, and fit. Boning helps support strapless dresses and to keep the fit of the bodice smooth.

Cap Sleeve: A short sleeve that covers the shoulder and the very top of the upper arm.

Color Blocking: In fashion, color blocking is when a garment is assembled using bold, contrasting colored "blocks" of fabric to create its form. Color blocking fabric was made popular during the '60s Mod fashion era.

Corset: A form-fitting top or undergarment with stiff, vertical boning support. Corsets can be worn to make a fashion statement or to cinch the waist under other fitted garments.

Circle Skirt: Literally, a circle of fabric where the hole in the center forms the waistline and gives lots of volume without any gathering or pleating at the waist. This is how poodle skirts are cut.

Cuff: The edge of a sleeve or pant leg. Cuff often refers to a fold of extra fabric on a pant leg or sleeve.

Empire Waist: The style of a dress or top where the waistline is placed high up under the bust.

Godet: A triangular piece of fabric sewn into a garment to add fullness. Godets are also referred to as gores or gussets.

14

Hemline: The bottom edge of a garment. Mini skirts have short hemlines, and evening gowns have long hemlines. The term refers more to the length of a garment than the style of the actual hem, which can be sewn many different ways: overlocked, rolled edge, folded hem, and blind hem, to name a few.

Monochromatic: Colors belonging to the same color family, but in varying shades and hues.

Peplum: A skirt attached to a bodice or cropped jacket. A peplum can also be a flounce-like extension of a bodice that just covers the hips.

Pintucks: A small, narrow fold of fabric stitched and pressed to form a neat line. Pintucks are usually sewn in groups parallel to one another to give texture and structure to a garment.

Platform Heels: Also called platforms, this style of shoe has a thick sole at the front and a high heel at the back. Platforms were made popular in the '70s Disco fashion era, but they have made a comeback in recent years and are prominent in contemporary fashion.

Pleats: A method of adding structure and volume to fabric by doubling it back on itself and then stitching it in place. Pleats can be soft (unpressed) or sharp (pressed).

Raglan Sleeve: A sleeve cut from one piece of fabric that extends to the neckline and attaches to the garment in a diagonal seam from the underarm to the collar. This style is widely known as a "baseball shirt."

Ribbing: Also known as "rib knit," ribbing is a stretchy fabric with a distinct vertical pattern. Tank tops, sweatshirt cuffs and waistbands, and socks use ribbing to hold the garment snug against the body.

Ruching: Also referred to as "shirring," ruching is the gathering of fabric along a seamline that creates soft folds and even draping on a garment. Ruching is often seen along the hip seams of chiffon and silk gowns, as well as the side and waistline seams of some tees. Ruching helps create a slimming effect across the midsection.

Seamline: A straight or curved line of stitching that joins two pieces of fabric to form a garment. Princess seamlines travel vertically from shoulder to hemline, curving along the form of the body.

Topstitching: Decorative stitching on the outside of a garment. Topstitching usually runs parallel to a seam and is often seen on jeans and denim garments, stitched in gold or white. Topstitching is also seen on corsets, belts, and leather accessories.

Tulle: Fine net fabric usually made of silk or nylon. Tulle is most often used for veils, tutus, or full-skirted gowns.

Velour: Velvet's more casual cousin in the fabric world. Velour has a soft, fuzzy nap and can be used for both apparel and upholstery. Stretch velour is popular for loungewear and tracksuits.

Figure Proportions

In traditional figure drawing, the human body is rendered in proportion. That is, the arms, hands, legs, feet, and torso are always drawn relative to each other in terms of size and space. The average adult body is seven to eight heads tall. In fashion illustration, however, artistic license may be taken to better serve the representation of the clothes being drawn. Fashion figure illustrations often have extraordinarily long legs, tiny waists, and wide-set shoulders. Many designers adopt their own sketching style. Use the proportions shown here as a guideline, but feel free to exaggerate or change them as you see fit. You are the designer—follow your own unique vision!

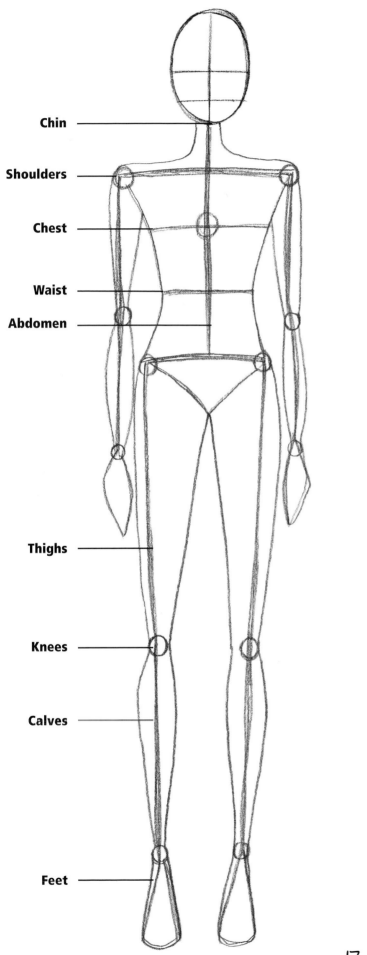

Chin

Shoulders

Chest

Waist

Abdomen

Thighs

Knees

Calves

Feet

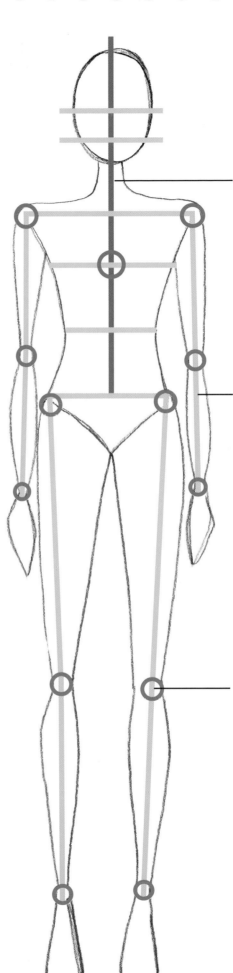

Midline –
The midline (shown in purple) is a vertical centerline that divides the body into identical left and right halves.

Gridlines –
Gridlines (shown in green) are horizontal and vertical lines that divide space and help determine proportion and scale. They are especially helpful in determining the placement of facial features.

Joints –
Use small circles (shown in pink) to indicate the joints at the shoulders, elbows, pelvis, wrists, knees, and ankles, as well as the chest.

17

Figure Poses

At times you will want to show your model from different angles. Maybe you've drawn a gown with a dramatic back that needs to be shown, or a side slit or other detail would be better represented from a profile view. Remember, the figure you draw is really only there as a "hanger" for the clothes. Choose the poses that best serve the garments.

Front   **Back**

Profile

Three-Quarter Back

Head + Face

In fashion illustration, the face is the least relevant part of the drawing. In fact, many designers don't even bother sketching more than an oval for the head and a bit of shading for the hair. Some designers might add more detail, but the sketchier you keep your figure, the more time you have to spend on the details of the garment.

Head Views For visual interest and variety, use different head positions in your drawings.

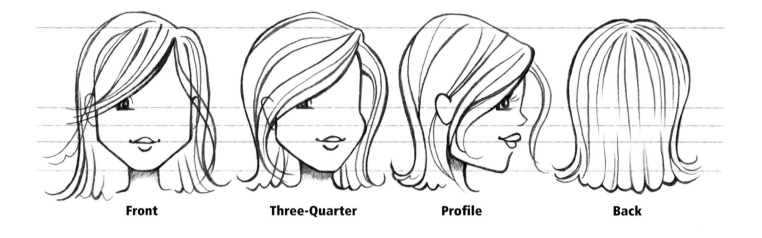

Front   **Three-Quarter**   **Profile**   **Back**

An Eye for Style

Notice the nonexistent noses and simplified eyes, lips, and ears. Even the hair consists of just a few basic lines to indicate shape and volume. This minimalist approach is favored in fashion drawing. Ears need only be an elongated C shape. In some cases, the nose can be omitted altogether. As you practice, you will develop your own way of drawing heads and faces that suits your personal style.

Eyes + Lips

A few strokes of the pencil are all it takes to indicate eyes. Thin brows are more feminine, while bushier brows add weight and translate to a masculine shape.

For lips, focus on drawing a full upper lip with just a small U shape below to indicate the shadow of a bottom lip. This gives the illusion of a pouty model.

Hairstyles

As with facial features, hairstyles can be indicated with just a few simple pencil lines. With slight modifications, you can create even more styles using the same basic techniques. For long, curly hair, sketch some vertical loops made with a very loose wrist. To show volume and height for smooth and shoulder-length hairstyles, use groups of closely spaced pencil lines. For braids, sketch in the basic curve first and then add alternating C shapes on either side of that guiding line to give a bit of texture. For men's hairstyles, a few angular, boxy lines and shading for sideburns will do the trick.

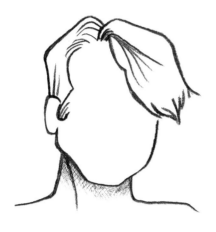

When sketching hairstyles, let your artistic instincts fly! Swoop hair across the eyes, or make it extra long, super spiky, or crazy full! The styling you add to your sketches enhances the clothing, and bold choices make for a more interesting result.

Arms + Hands

Hands can be tricky. If you don't need them in your pose, hide them in a pocket or behind the model's skirt or back. When a hand on the hip or in a pocket is necessary, simply indicate the shape and keep it simple—do not be concerned with articulating every finger and nail.

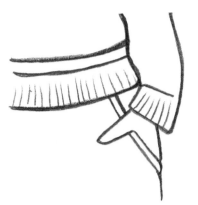

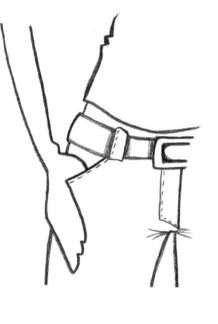

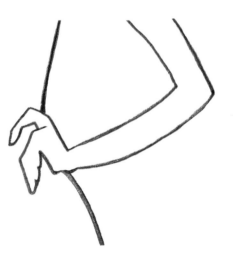

Hands On

Even when your model is holding an item like a clutch handbag, it isn't necessary to render the hands in great detail. Simply indicating the shape is enough to communicate the desired effect.

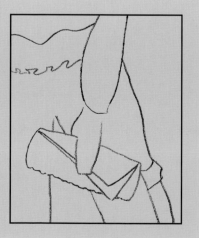

Legs + Feet

Feet are important in fashion because they show the shoes, which are often a big part of the design. Take some time to learn the basic angles of the feet, whether they are flat or in heels.

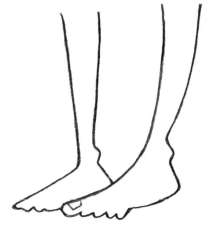

Hot to Trot

The most widely used pose—the classic "model" pose—features one elongated foot from the front/top angle and a foot positioned behind it at a side angle. The front foot is long, oval, and slightly "diamond" shaped; the back foot is a bit triangular shaped. Think of a wedge heel. This basic shape is the foundation for all high-heel styles.

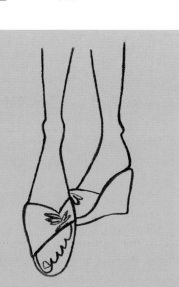

Using Mannequins

For quick sketches of simple garments—
or on days when you just feel like getting
to the good stuff—you may want to
skip drawing a model and sketch on a
mannequin or dress form. You can use
these two forms—one male, one female—
again and again to whip out cute designs
that don't require a lot of fuss. This is a
great way to show a series of designs or
variations of a simple design. To practice
creating designs using these mannequins
and other figure poses, turn to page 111
for loads of traceable templates.

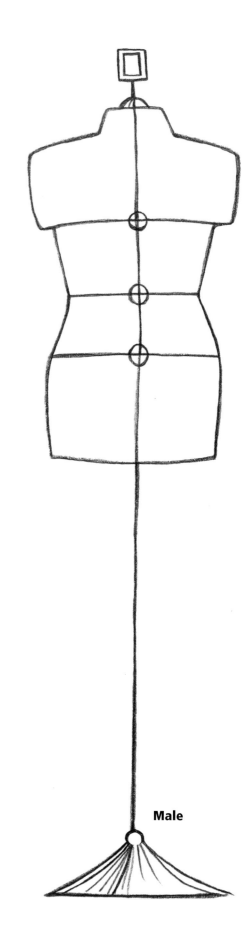

Female

Male

Fashion Drawing Tips + Tricks

If your design is feeling like more erasing than sketching, stop and start over with a fresh piece of paper.

Do not color your original line drawings. Instead, make a clean tracing of your drawing and then add color to that. It's always good to have the styles you've created available for future use, especially if you want to experiment with different colors and textures.

Don't reinvent the wheel. There are no fashion police! If you love a certain silhouette you've created, there's no rule saying you can't use it again and again with different colors or details.

Create a "you" illustration with your look, coloring, and hairstyle. Trace this figure whenever you feel like designing for yourself. It's amazing how much easier you will find the design process when you feel like you are actually dressing yourself. Certain details will just look right.

Don't feel like you need to color the model every time. Leaving the model in pencil and simply coloring or shading the garment helps keep the focus where it needs to be—on the clothes.

Force yourself to sketch quickly. Often, the best shapes and styles come when you are not trying too hard and laboring over every line. Let the basic silhouette of your design flow out of your hand in a few quick swoops; then go back and refine. You will like the final outcome of these drawings much better.

Take risks! These are just drawings, so go ahead and use bold color, mix patterns, and play with scale. Erasers and fresh paper are a simple solution if you make a mistake. But try to let your personality and signature style show through!

Think of garment construction and wearability while sketching. The clothes you design ultimately need to be created and sewn. Strapless dresses need boning to stay up and sometimes you will need a seam where you wish you didn't. But keeping the creation of your garments in mind when sketching will save you a lot of disappointment later if you want to create real clothes from your designs.

Chapter 2

Garments, Shoes + Accessories

Tops, Tees & Tanks

Crew Neck

Scoop Neck

Polo Shirt

V Neck

Button-down Short Sleeve

Empire Waist

Tank Top

Spaghetti Strap Tank

Scoop Neck Sleeveless

Halter Top

Wraparound

Button-down Long Sleeve

Jeans, Pants + Shorts

Denim Cutoffs

Cuffed

Capris

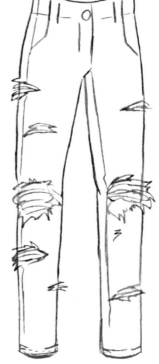

Distressed Jeans

Drawstring

Sweat Shorts

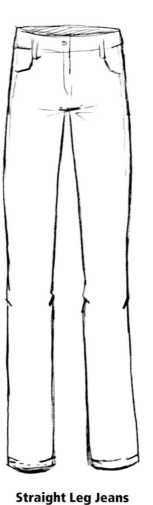

Straight Leg Jeans

Bootcut Jeans

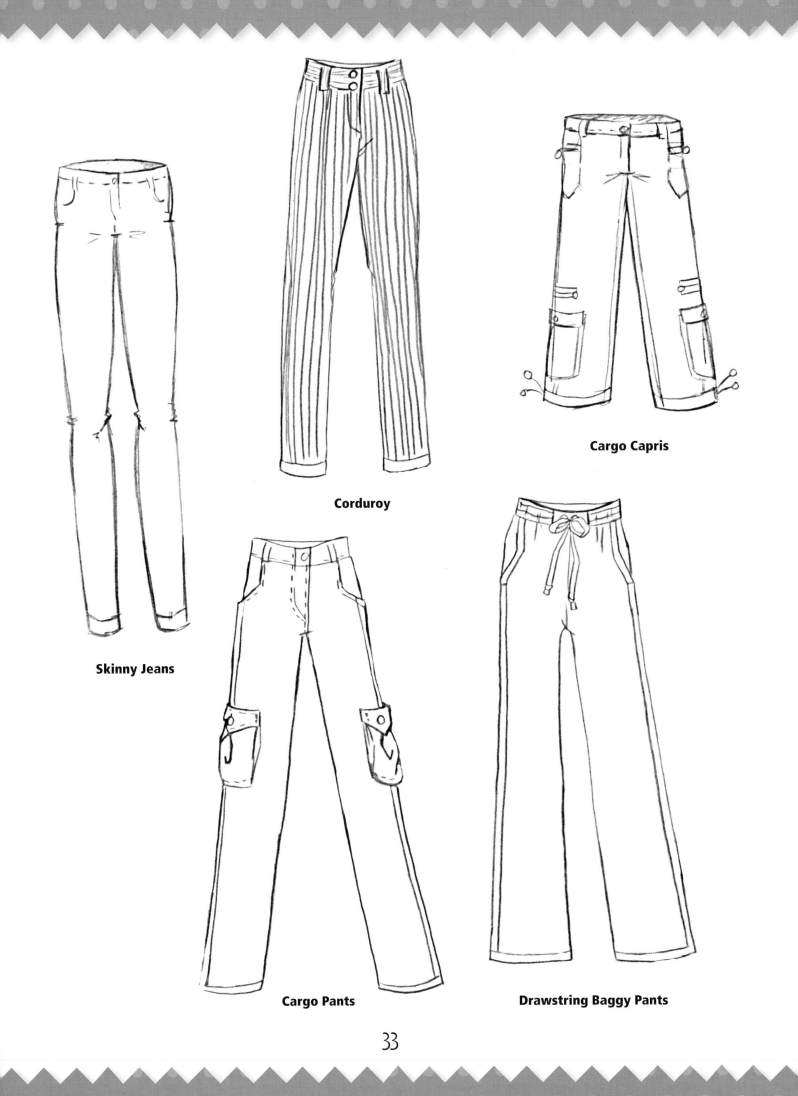

Corduroy

Cargo Capris

Skinny Jeans

Cargo Pants

Drawstring Baggy Pants

Skirts, Dresses + Gowns

Ruffle Skirt

Balloon Skirt

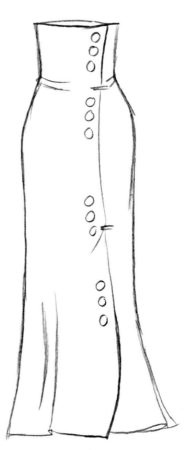

High-waist Skirt

Pleated Skirt

Draped Skirt

A-Line Skirt

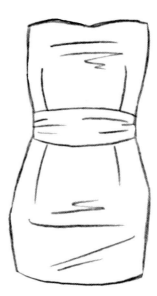

Strapless Mini Dress

Sundress

V Neck Dress

Pleated Halter Dress

Shirt Dress

Strapless Gown

Mermaid Gown

Sleeveless Gown with Slit

35

Sweaters, Jackets + Outerwear

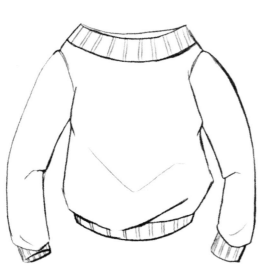

Pullover

Button-down Cableknit

Button-down Cardigan

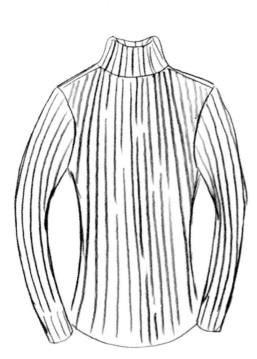

Ribbed Turtleneck

Poncho

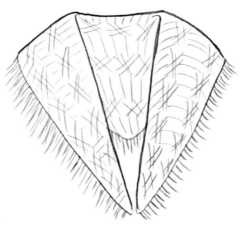

Shawl

Faux Fur Coat

Zip-up Hoodie

Hooded Sweatshirt

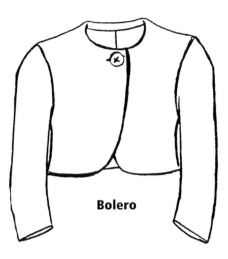

Bolero

Peacoat

Ski Jacket

Blazer

Trench Coat

Hats

Headscarf

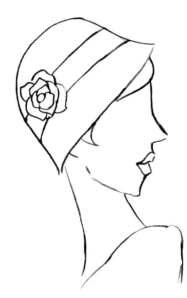

Cloche

Newsboy Cap

Knit Cap

Stocking Cap

Cowboy Hat

Sun Hat

Ski Cap

Wide Brim Hat

Bucket Hat

Shoes + Handbags

Flats

Ankle Boot

Open-toe Heel Sandal

Stiletto

Flip-flops

Sneaker

Wedge

Peep-toe Pump

Knee-high Boots

Rain Boots

40

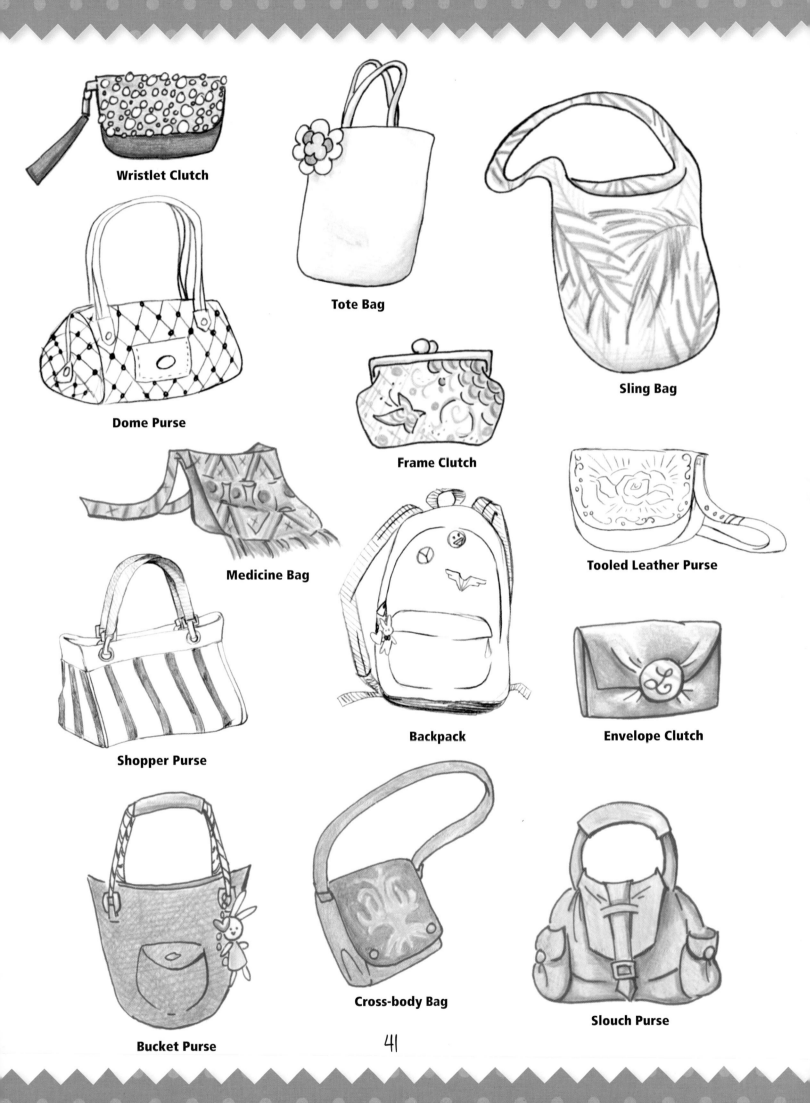

Wristlet Clutch

Tote Bag

Sling Bag

Dome Purse

Frame Clutch

Medicine Bag

Tooled Leather Purse

Shopper Purse

Backpack

Envelope Clutch

Bucket Purse

Cross-body Bag

Slouch Purse

41

Chapter 3

Current Fashion Styles

Chic + Trendy

Imagine a bustling street in the middle of New York City—fashion capital of the world. Our chic and trendy girl exudes style and confidence. She knows what's hot in the world of fashion, and she has the wardrobe to prove it! In fact, she's about ready to hit Fifth Avenue for a day-long shopping spree at her favorite designer boutiques.

1

Draw a stick figure in the general shape of the model's stance. Use the Figure Proportion guidelines on pages 16–17 to help you, if necessary.

2

Begin to add volume to the body and limbs. The easiest way to do this is to draw the joints as circles and then draw connecting lines from one circle to the next. Use horizontal lines for the bust, waist, and hips. Block in loose shapes for the hands and feet.

3

Now add gridlines to the face, and use light sketch lines to rough in the shapes of the clothes and hair. Feel free to play with the pant length, the position of the cargo pockets, and the volume of the sleeves on the top. Draw the shape of the shoes. Rough in long, loose waves of hair to go with the cool, casual vibe of the clothes. Hair like this consists of only a few scribbles. Have fun!

4

Now darken your final sketch lines and erase stray marks.

5

Start adding the facial features, such as a one-eye/pouty lips combo. Our girl's layered necklaces are rendered with light pencil strokes and some small circles for beads. Draw in double-lined edges to indicate topstitching on the cargo pants. Then add gathers at the pant legs to show ruching at the outer seams. Add lace detail at the waist by filling in the scalloped edge with simple shapes. Draw the plaid pattern on the shoes following the contour of the foot.

6

Art markers are great for creating a bold look or saturated color. Sweep the color on in broad strokes. Use overlapping strokes to capture a sketchy feel. Sketchier shading in the pants shows their crisp texture. Lay down the base color of the shoes with marker; then use a gel pen and colored pencil to overlay the gridlines of the plaid.

For a realistic color final, apply shading just under the chin, cuffs, and hemlines. This adds depth and dimension.

Girly + Romantic

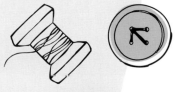

Girly and romantic style is all about muted tones and soft textures. This girl loves the color pink, lace, ribbons, frills, ruffles, and pretty flowers—especially in her hair. She looks radiant in a sheer, flowing dress, and she almost always wears her long hair down in loose, springy curls.

1

This figure is drawn at a three-quarter angle to show off the side detail of her dress. Because this model is barefoot, draw the feet flat on the ground.

2

Add volume to the body and limbs. Remember to indicate the shoulders, elbows, wrist, knees, and feet with small circles. Then connect the circles with light pencil lines to form the limbs. This figure is a bit more challenging because of the angles of her head, neck, and torso. Posing in front of a mirror may help you establish the angles of the bustline, shoulderline, and waistline.

3

Sketch light gridlines on the face. With a loose, light hand, rough in the structure of the clothes. Use light strokes to capture thin, airy fabrics, such as chiffon. This garment is form-fitting on top and loose on the bottom. Feel free to exaggerate the length of the hair. (Think Rapunzel!) Fashion drawings should inspire!

4

Darken your final sketch lines and erase strays, or use a light box and tracing paper. (See "How to Use a Light Box," page 9.)

5

Now give this romantic girl lush lashes and full lips. Add a locket (which is surely hiding a photo of her love). Draw in stacks of beaded bracelets and flowers in her long hair, and create the lace slips by drawing sketchy scallop marks under the hemline. Double up the seamlines in the corset to indicate boning and topstitching. Use light pencil marks to indicate the shirred chiffon of the bodice overlay that gathers at the shoulder. Draw the beading under the bust using clusters of small, imperfect circles.

6

The key to getting a soft, ethereal look is to layer in color. Use watercolor washes or a very pale marker to get a slight blush of color laid down. Then use a light touch to add in monochromatic tones. Start by laying down color with the lightest hue in the color family of your choosing; then gradually work up to the shadows on the folds using the darkest tones in creases and gathers.

To capture the transparency of the chiffon, add the skin color first. Then lightly color over it with your fabric color. Use a sienna or dark-toned pencil to indicate shadow in appropriate places, such as under the chin and at the hemline.

Fun + Casual

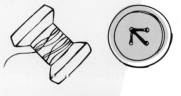

A fun and casual style is often seen on the fresh-faced girl next door. She's sweet, down-to-earth, and friends with just about everybody. Although this gal isn't opposed to dressing up when the occasion calls for it, she is most comfortable wearing jeans, a skinny tee, and her favorite sneakers. She also goes easy on the makeup.

1

This girl's pose matches her personality: laid back and approachable. Begin by roughing in a simple stick figure, positioning the feet shoulder-width apart.

2

Add volume to the form by drawing small circles at the joints and then connecting them to form the limbs. Sketch the thumbs hooked into the pockets, but don't spend too much time on the hands and feet. Just use broad shapes.

3

Add gridlines to the face and a midline to help with the placement of the facial features. Swipe in a cute chin-length bob and a stylish ensemble of jeans, skinny tee, and low-top sneakers. Feel free to crop the tee and play with the length of the jeans.

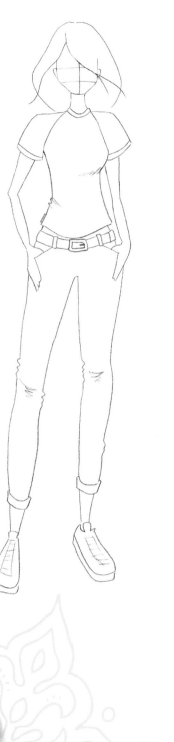

4

Erase stray pencil lines or unwanted marks.

5

Start bringing your outfit to life by filling in the details. Add a logo to the tee—real or imagined—and refine the details on the belt. Don't forget to add the topstitching detail to the jeans. To achieve the look, draw a dashed line down the length of each outer pant-leg seam. Add the stitching to the zipper fly and belt loops, and fill in the details of the shoes. These little elements make all the difference. A pair of dangly earrings brings up the style quotient, as does a wide-eyed gaze and slight smile.

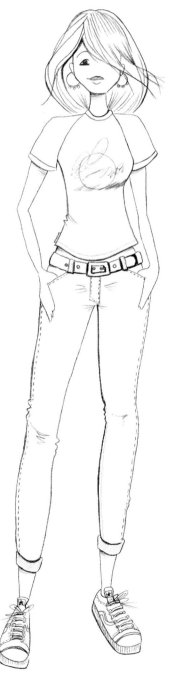

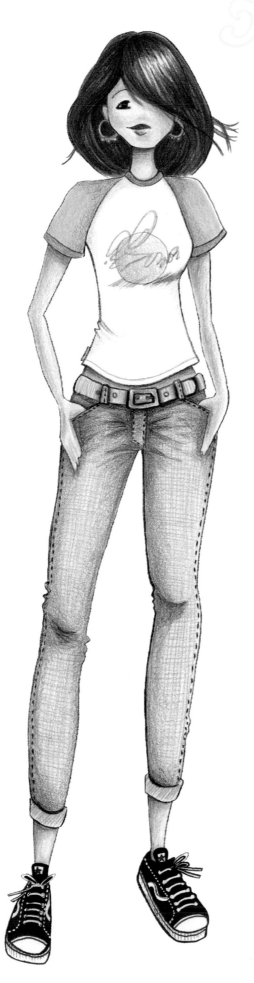

6

Use art markers for the base color and colored pencil or pens for the details and accents. Use green-gray as the base color for the jeans, with a bit of blue pencil to shade in key areas. You can achieve the texture of the jeans by crosshatching fine lines along the length of each leg. (See "Hatching," page 10.) Add shadows at the knees and seams by darkening the color. Use a bold color for the belt to up the fun. A white gel pen is perfect for rendering the topstitching on the black sneakers. Use a metallic gel pen if you want to make the earrings and belt buckle shimmer a bit. Remember to shade the skin at places where there is a bit of shadow, including under the chin, sleeves, and pant legs.

Although the tee is mostly white, it's been accented with a muted periwinkle in places where a shadow would be cast. It helps the garment read as white and not just unfinished.

Confident + Classic

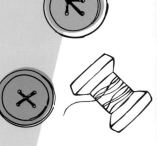

This no-nonsense gal has it all going on, and it shows in her posture and sophisticated sense of style. She is smart, sassy, and ready to take on anything that the day—and the world—has in store for her. Look for her to be perfectly accessorized every time she steps foot out of the front door.

Sketch a rough stick figure in a "power" pose: hand on the hip, one foot in front of the other with a slight bend in the knee, back leg straight, and super high heels!

Add volume to the body, noting that the shoulders for this figure are squared. Connect your circles with sweeping lines to shape the arms and legs. Draw horizontal lines across the torso at the lower bustline, waist, and hips. You've got one classy figure there!

Draw a light midline down the center of the face and gridlines at the eyes and mouth. Rough in the shapes of the clothes and hair. The shape of her hair shows a perfect salon blowout: It's got volume, a soft flip, and sweeping bangs. This figure's clothes are sleek, streamlined, and tailored—a more feminine version of the "power suit." Be creative with the neckline and design details. The pencil skirt and stilettos complete her look.

4

Darken final sketch lines and erase any unwanted marks.

5

Begin adding accessories and facial features. Start with this gal's face, and the rest will follow. A perfectly arched brow and bow lips are confidence personified. The best fashion drawings are all about the cute details. Draw the gathered cap sleeves by adding tiny lines at the sleeve hem. This creates the illusion of folds. Draw a few flared sections on the peplum at the hip, as well as a skinny belt. Add a subtle swipe of color blocking across the bodice for a clean, finished look. Add some pearls at the neck and wrist.

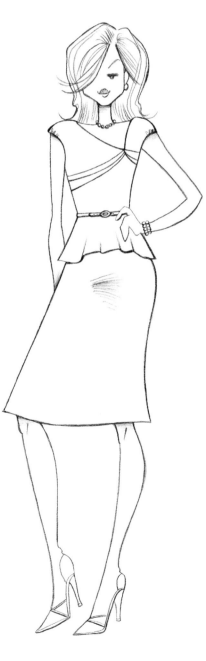

6

Choose a strong color like red for this outfit, but be sure to use different shades to give the final art depth and drama. The base color is true red, while burgundy and plum shading create a richer hue. The color-blocked panels in the bodice are darkened in with the same colors. Shading around the folds in the peplum make them pop. To keep the outfit looking classy, the shoes and belt are nude colored. (A chic girl always has some great neutral-colored shoes in her arsenal!) Accent the pearls with a touch of gray-blue to make the white stand out. Then finish the hair in a deep, rich tone. Remember to shade the skin in places where the clothing casts a shadow—it will really elevate your drawing.

Highlights can add a polished look to your final drawing. Notice how a couple of simple lines rendered on the skirt with the tip of a white marker add an elegant finishing touch.

Athletic + Sporty

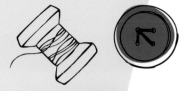

Whether she's in the gym, shooting hoops, or running track, this athlete always works out in style. But even when she's taking a breather, she loves hanging out in fun and flirty velour sweatsuits. Check her closet and you'll find that she has one of every color—with athletic footwear to match!

You know the "comfy sweats" pose—it's easy and relaxed. Draw a basic stick figure, keeping to the proportional guide. This model will be wearing athletic shoes, so make sure to draw the feet flat.

 2

Once again, sketch circles to indicate the joints; then add horizontal lines at chest, waist, and hips to form the torso. Connect these guidelines with light pencil strokes to form the body.

 3

Draw a midline down the center of the face and then sketch in horizontal lines for eyes and mouth. Rough in the outline for the shape of the hair, which is—appropriately—in pigtails. Begin drawing in the sweats using flowy lines that loosely follow the body contours. The softer the curves, the better.

4

Darken your outlines, and erase unnecessary sketch marks.

5

This is one happy girl. After all, who doesn't like to be in comfy clothes? Add a cute smile and twinkle in her eye. Sketch in a darker top lip for depth. She is a simple girl, so keep accessories basic: a tiny gold pendant and sneakers peeking out from under wide-legged sweatpants. Add pockets and a matching design.

6

Choose a cheerful color that will enhance the depth of the velour texture. I started with a light aqua marker and then worked up the tones with turquoise, teal, and electric blue for the deepest areas of shading. Use a light touch and multi-directional strokes to keep the texture looking soft and "velvety." Add some punches of color to the graphics on the garments, as well as at the tip of the sneakers. Then add just a bit of shading to the skin to finish the look.

Try drawing one or both of the figure's hands behind the back or in pockets. Some designers skip drawing hands altogether. The important part is the clothes, so hands should be loosely indicated, not labored over.

Bohemian + Eclectic

Our boho girl is earthy and cool. She might be an artist, poet, or dog walker, but she uses fashion to express her personality. She loves to mix and match colors and exotic textures, and she's not afraid to pair haute couture with a funky vintage find that she scored at a thrift store. She's the girl who can pull off looks that nobody else can.

1

Sketch a stick figure in a walking stance.

2

Draw small circles to indicate the joints; then draw connecting lines from one circle to the next to indicate the arms and legs. Add horizontal lines at the bust, waist, and hips. Block in loose geometric shapes for the hands and feet.

3

Draw a light midline and gridlines on the face to help with feature placement. Use a light hand to rough in the clothing. This model is wearing a lot of layers, including a form-fitting shirt, long jacket, and scarf. Indicate the rips in the jeans and rough in the boots, which stop about midcalf. Finally, sketch in long, naturally wavy hair with a couple of lines to indicate what will be the loose braids.

4

Tighten the details and darken the final sketch lines; then erase stray marks.

5

Continue to refine the details of the outfit and add in the facial features. The patchwork jacket has exposed seams that reveal sherpa fur. Fun shapes give the patches on the jeans character and an opportunity to add color. The skinny scarf with sequin trim and dangly earrings lend an exotic touch. Slouchy boots with multiple straps and buckles are perfect for this gal.

66

6

This style is full of natural textures, as well as whimsical accents and accessories. Color the coat carefully in marker, leaving the fur bits white. Layer in matching colored pencil in light swirls all over the jacket to soften the color and create a suede-like texture. Crosshatching on the jeans and boots helps them look weathered, natural, and broken in. She's über cool without even trying.

Too add depth and dimension to longer hair, start light and build up color with two or three layers of colored pencil.

Rebellious + Daring

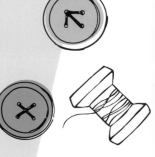

Don't judge a book by its cover. This daring diva may have a tough exterior, but she's a sweetheart on the inside. She's not afraid to speak her mind, especially to defend those who can't defend themselves. She's often misunderstood because of her style preference, but she won't change for anyone because she knows exactly who she is!

1

Sketch a simple stick figure in a casual pose, with ankles crossed and the chin resting on the hand.

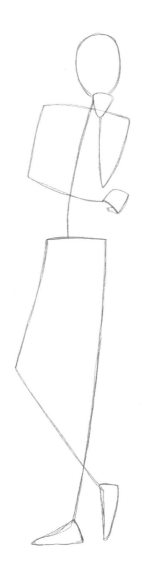

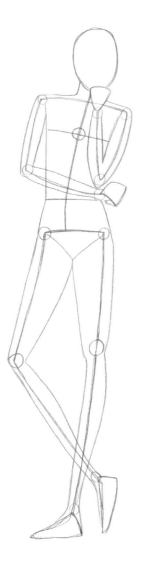

2

Sketch circles to indicate the joint positions; then connect them to form the limbs.

3

Sketch a light grid on the face to indicate the positioning of the features. With a loose hand, rough in the shape of the clothes. Sharp angles and straight lines will help with drawing the structured leather jacket. Be bold, but don't overdo the clothes on this character. She's as un-fussy as they come!

4

Darken final sketch lines and erase strays. Tighten up the details of the clothing, hair, and shoes.

5

Start adding in the facial features, making sure to give this girl dark, angular lashes and a slight smirk. Add stud earrings and retro gym socks peeking over some high-top combat boots. Camouflage cargo pants are a must—you can create the pattern by drawing splotchy shapes that look similar to jigsaw-puzzle pieces. Zippers on the jacket add personality, and layered tees peeking from under the motorcycle jacket are all that's needed to complete this tough-girl look.

6

This girl may have a rebellious streak, but she still uses color to express herself. Resist the urge to use only black! Remember, fashion design is fun and freeing, so don't be afraid of color. The motorcycle jacket is dark navy with white racing stripes, and the boots are dark green. Leave some highlights on the boots to show their shine. The camouflage should be subtle, so use a light hand and colored pencil in similar shades of "army" green and brown to create the pattern. A spunky purple streak in the spiky hair is the perfect crowning touch to this rebel with a cause.

Look through fashion magazines or clothing catalogs to find interesting model poses. Models know exactly how to show off clothes, which is what you're trying to do in your drawings.

Skater Dude

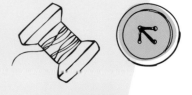

This guy was practically born riding a skateboard. He spends almost all of his free time at the local skate park showing off his ollies, heelflips, and noseslides. But our skater guy doesn't just talk the talk—he's got more board shorts than he does pants, and he wears a different skater tee almost every day of the month.

1

The shape of this figure will be broader and more squared; however, you can still follow the same general proportions as you did for the female figures. Just drop the waist and hips a bit, and draw a wider shoulder line. Position the legs and feet in a firm, grounded stance.

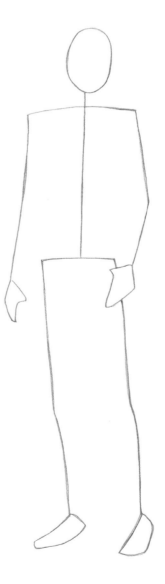

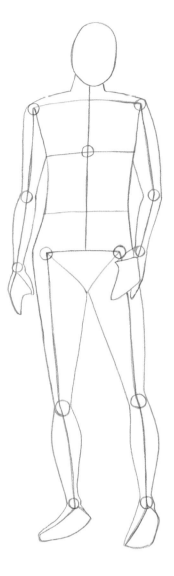

 2

Add volume to the form by drawing circles at the joints and connecting them to form the limbs. Feel free to broaden the limbs when connecting them so that they have some weight and strength.

3

Sketch a light midline down the center of the face, as well as horizontal lines at the eyes and mouth. Indicate sideburns and hair using angular lines, which also conveys masculinity. A simple, fitted tee; long, baggy board shorts; and casual, slip-on skate shoes complete the look.

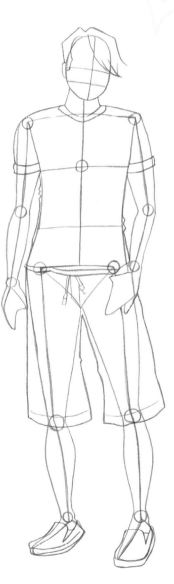

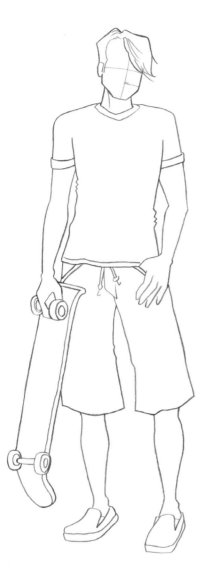

4

Erase unwanted sketch lines and refine the details. Then bring out this guy's "too-cool-for-school" personality by adding his prized skateboard.

5

Now it's time to give this guy a little style. A ringer tee, brightly patterned shorts, and a bold graphic on the skateboard amp up his urban appeal.

6

Use art markers to add bold color and smooth textures. Overlapping the broad marker strokes in the shirt gives the illusion of wide ribbing in the knit; shading at the sides adds contour. Bright shorts are fine, but temper them with neutral shoes and a muted (but matching) shirt.

When using bold colors, think about what is fashionable and what a real person would wear. This will prevent your drawing from appearing unrealistic or cartoon-like.

Chapter 4

Fabulous Fashions from History

'40s Swing

Swanky yet demure, this circa 1940s swing gal rocks it every time she jitterbugs, jives, shimmies, snaps, taps, and strolls her way across the dance floor. A cosmopolitan girl, she can be seen twirling around with a well-dressed fella in a Zoot suit five nights a week. In between songs, you'll find her in a booth sipping Shirley Temples—with two cherries.

1

Sketch a simple stick figure with one hip slightly raised.

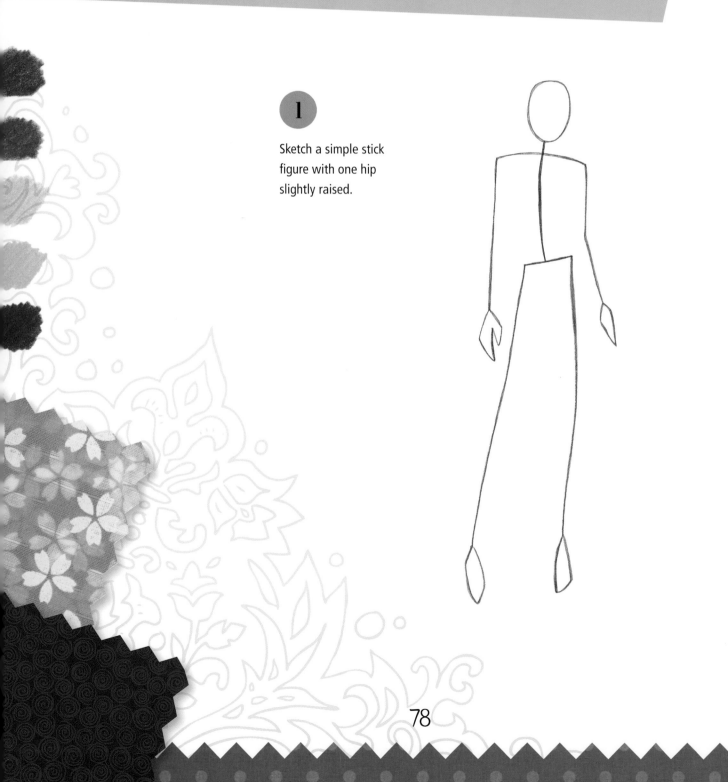

2

Rough in the joints and limbs. This pose is symmetrical and crisp, which will make the clothes look all the better.

3

Draw a light midline and horizontal gridlines on the face. Then start roughing in the shape of the dress. This model's hair is parted in the center with rolled waves tucked neatly in place. The flower on the belt, T-strap heels, chiffon godets in the skirt, and gathers at the bustline are perfectly in sync with this decade's fashion.

4

Darken the final sketch lines and erase strays. Then refine the details of the dress and shoes.

5

This gal has a perfectly manicured brow and full lips. Start adding in more details, including center seams and gathering in the skirt insets using long, sweeping lines. Add a chunky bracelet to go along with matching stud earrings.

6

With the exception of the godets, lay in the base color of the dress evenly with navy marker. Then fill in the godets with navy colored pencil, which will help indicate the sheer texture of the material. Apply red marker evenly on the belt, leaving small gaps of white to give the look of patent leather. Repeat this process on the shoes. No proper swing gal would ever mismatch her shoes and belt! Finally, use a white pencil sharpened to a crisp point to add the polka dots. Move slowly and work in even rows until the entire dress is filled. Be patient! You will love the pattern when it's complete.

Consult books or online photo references to get a feel for the clothes from this era. Flowing, below-the-knee skirts and fitted, seamed bodices are the hallmarks of 1940s glamour.

'50s Rock 'n' Roll

In a pink wool poodle skirt, monogrammed pullover cardigan, black-and-white saddle shoes, and neckerchief, our '50s gal is right and ready for the local sock hop. She likes sipping root beer floats at the soda fountain after school and going to the roller rink on Friday nights. She also dreams of owning a powder-pink Cadillac convertible.

1

Rough sketch the pose. Although this model's hands will be behind her back in the final step, it's important to draw them anyway, so that the pose feels proportional and authentic.

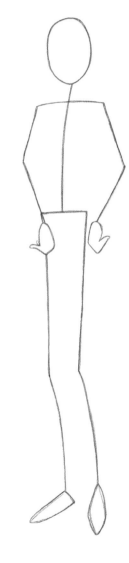

2

Rough in the joints, limbs, and gridlines.

3

Draw a light midline and horizontal gridlines for the eyes and mouth. The horizontal lines are especially helpful for this model because they will help you determine the length of her bangs. Rough in the outline of the hair and ponytail. Then block in the shapes of the fitted sweater and circle skirt. Finally, add the outline of a poodle to the front of the skirt.

4

Darken final sketch lines and erase stray marks. Refine the sketch of the poodle, adding a pearl collar for panache and a long, curly line for the leash.

5

Draw an initial appliqué on the shoulder, a neckerchief, and the classic black-and-white saddle shoes. Indicate ribbing at sweater hem and sleeves with short, swift pencil strokes.

6

The only rule here is to choose cheerful colors. Lay in a base color on the skirt using art markers. Top it off with a coordinating colored pencil applied in even, swirling loops to get a velvety texture indicative of the wool used most often for poodle skirts. Use a similar method for the sweater. A bit of blue or gray shading on the white of the poodle's fur and the saddle shoes gives depth and shadow. Add peach for the skin tone and pink for the lips.

To give the hair a hint of sheen, use a fine-tipped white marker or white pencil to add a few understated highlights near the top front of the head.

'60s Mod Squad

A color-blocked, shift mini dress paired with go-go boots epitomized this fashion movement, also known as "Mod"—short for modern. Dressed in a clean, crisp silhouette consistent with the times, this cool gal loves to attend poetry readings and drink espresso at the local coffeehouse.

1

Sketch a simple stick figure standing face forward—the perfect pose in which to capture the bold symmetry of this clothing style.

2

Sketch small circles to indicate the joint positions, and draw a small inverted triangle for the pelvis. Then draw horizontal gridlines to indicate the bust and waist. These lines will come in handy when you start designing the geometric, color blocking of the dress. Fill in the volume of the arms and legs, adding rudimentary shapes to indicate hands and feet.

3

Add faint gridlines and a vertical midline to the face. Rough in the basic shape of the clothing and hair. This garment has a simple, body-conscious silhouette and crisp lines. Go-go boots are a must, as is a bobbed hairstyle.

4

Darken your final sketch lines and erase any strays.

5

Now add the facial features and tighten up the A-line dress, which sports a high waistline and funnel collar. A simple cuff bracelet and a wide-eyed stare with a bit of graphic eye makeup complete this look.

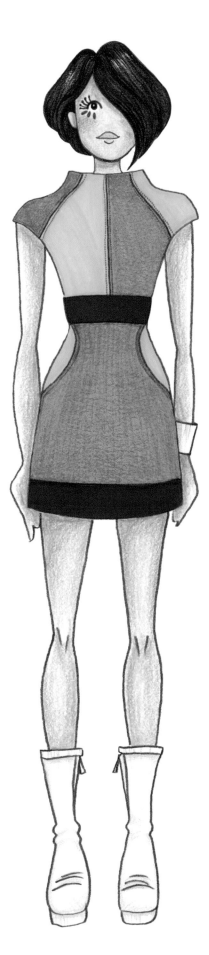

6

Start with art markers to lay in contrasting bright hues in a color-blocked pattern. You can accentuate the smooth texture by softly going over the marker with the same color of pencil. Add a bit of pale-blue shading to the go-go boots to enhance their white color—because all self-respecting go-go boots have got to be shiny and white!

The fashions of the '60s were known for their bright, colorful patterns. Feel free to mix and match bold colors, and incorporate geometric shapes into your designs.

'70s Disco

Long before "bling" became a buzzword, the Disco movement had the cornerstone on flashy style. Glitter, sparkles, sequins, and gold were mainstays in fashion, and body-hugging outfits combined with platform shoes lit up every multicolored dance floor in town. Our '70s girl, a self-proclaimed dancing queen, definitely has an eye for style.

1

Sketch in a simple stick figure.

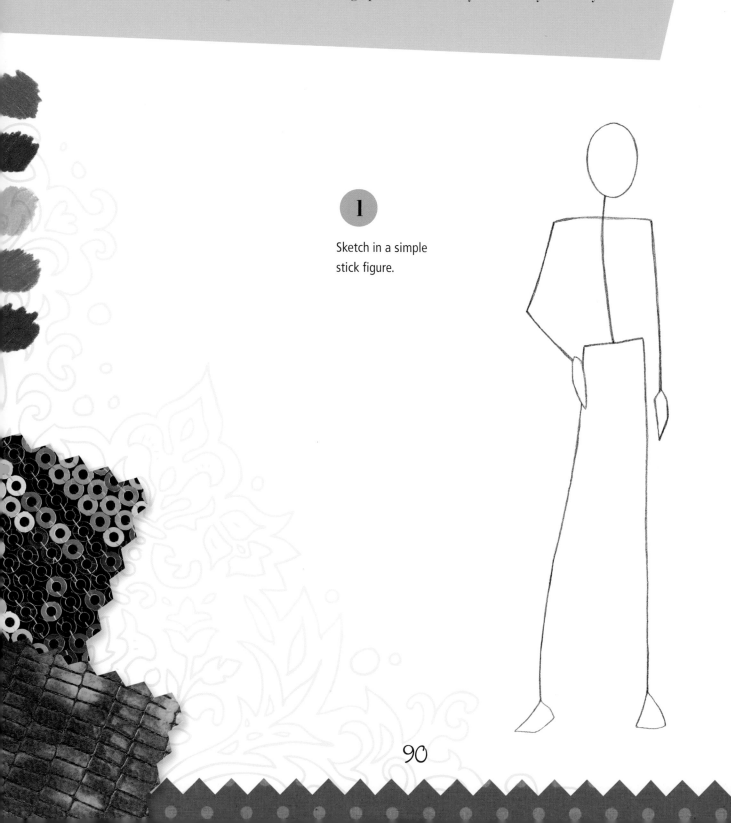

2

Indicate the joints by sketching circles at the elbow, knee, and ankle positions. Then connect the circles with light pencil lines to form the limbs. Disco style is all about curves, so don't be afraid to add a bit of roundness and volume as you connect the circles. This outfit will hug the shape of the figure.

3

Now rough in gridlines for the face and an outline for the hair. Sketch in the shape of the outfit through the torso, as well as folds at the hemline of the bell-bottoms to suggest flowing fabric. A plunging, halter-style neckline is spot-on for this era. Don't forget to suggest platform shoes peeking out from under the pant legs.

4

Erase unnecessary sketch lines, and darken your final outline.

5

Disco style is practically synonymous with sparkle and pizzazz. Add a braided headband at the temple, a low-slung beaded belt at the hip, brazen platform shoes, and a necklace with a medallion. Complete the look by adding some ruching on the bodice, as well as feathered hair.

6

Pick a fun color for the jumpsuit and go to town with your art markers. Overlapping the strokes in the bodice and folds of the pant hems will give the illusion of volume. You can smooth out any streaks and add a bit of contour by overlaying the whole jumpsuit with a colored pencil one shade darker. Choose a fiery red for the hair, and then layer in other shades of red for depth. A few twinkly stars made with white gel pen among the beads in the belt will convey sparkle. And, yes, light blue eye shadow is definitely allowed!

A few strokes of the pencil and a bit of bold color are all you need to suggest shoes. The viewer doesn't need to see an entire shoe to get a sense of its shape and style.

'80s New Wave

Girls just want to have fun! The '80s were defined by all things big and bold: big hair, big jewelry, bold colors, and—of course—a big, bold attitude. And this New Wave girl has it all and then some. This style knows no rules and no boundaries. It's mixing and matching at its best: a fluffy petticoat, corseted top over a tee, fishnet leggings, fingerless gloves, and high-heeled booties paired with ruffled socks create a totally awesome style suited for the girl who is truly self-confident.

1

Start by sketching a stick figure in a wide stance with one leg turned out.

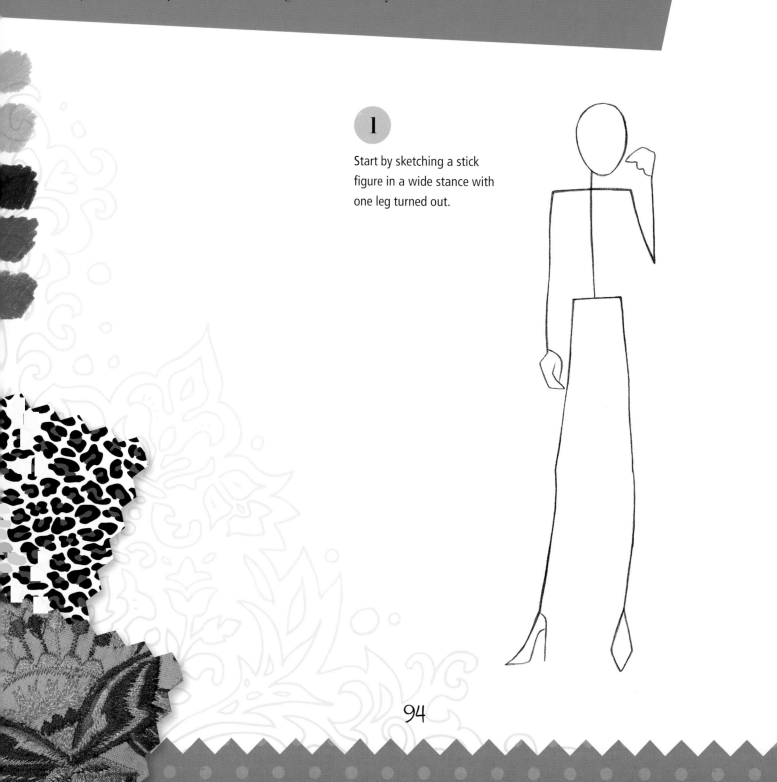

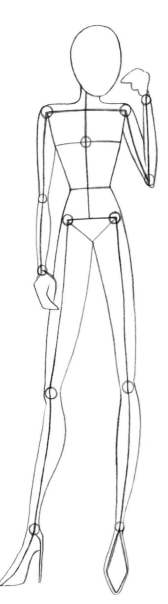

2

Add volume by sketching circles at the joints; then connect the circles to form limbs. Add horizontal lines at the chest and waist to fill in the torso.

3

Draw a faint vertical midline down the center of the face; then add horizontal lines at the eyes and mouth. Begin sketching in the outfit and hair.

4

Erase unnecessary sketch marks, and darken your final outlines.

5

Begin filling in the details, including boning to the corset; a wide, lace headband; chunky earrings; and loads of bracelets on one arm. Use loose, squiggly lines to indicate the gathered tulle petticoat; then add crosshatching to capture the fishnet detail of the tights and gloves. Now sketch in the necklaces, more layers of spiky hair, and the remaining detail of the booties.

6

Use art markers to render the bright neon hues; colored pencils to shade in the corset, tee, and shoes; and a fine-tipped black pigment pen to add thin crosshatching in the petticoat. Go crazy with color in the hair.

When it comes to color for '80s fashions, anything goes. Almost every pattern and print from the era looks as if it got in the way of a box of exploding crayons!

Chapter 5

Custom Designs

Renaissance Era

Fashion designers aren't limited to designing strictly for the runway. In fact, many professionals prefer designing costumes for the performing arts, such as the theater, opera, and ballet, or for movies and television. This costume channels none other than the damsel Juliet from William Shakespeare's famous tragedy, *Romeo and Juliet*.

1

Sketch a forward-facing stick figure.

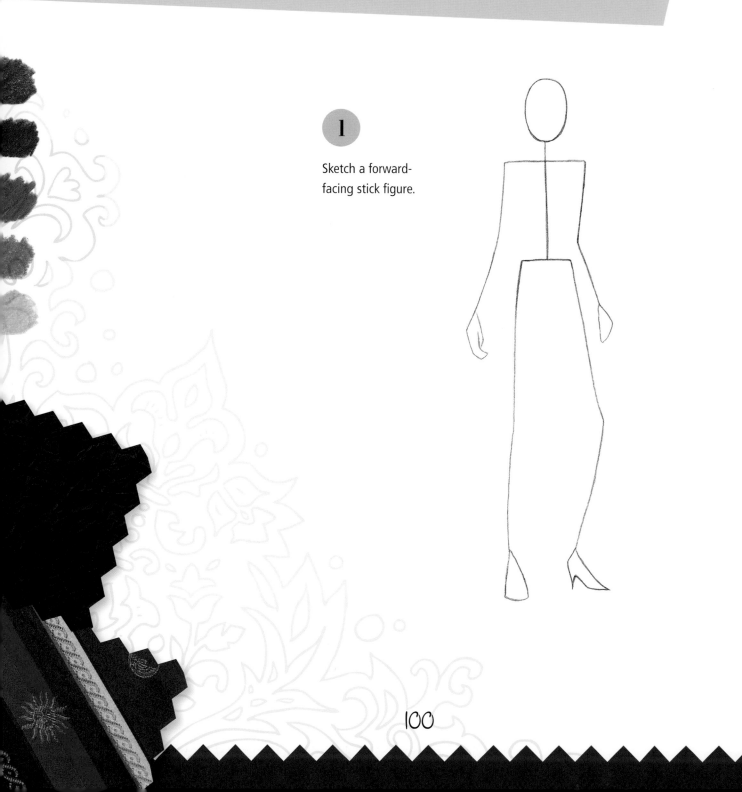

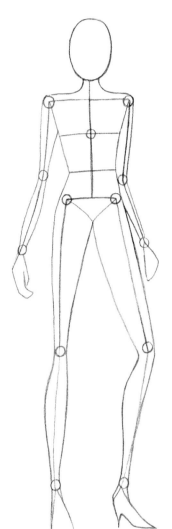

 2

Draw small circles at the joints and then connect them to each other to fill out the arms, legs, and torso. This Renaissance-era maiden is slight and demure.

 3

Add a light vertical midline down the center of the face and horizontal gridlines to indicate the positions of the features. Draw an outline of long hair tied into a sectioned ponytail. The maiden's garment features light gauzy fabrics with lots of gathering and volume. The sleeve detail is soft and dramatic, and the empire waist evokes the period. A traditional ruffle completes the hem.

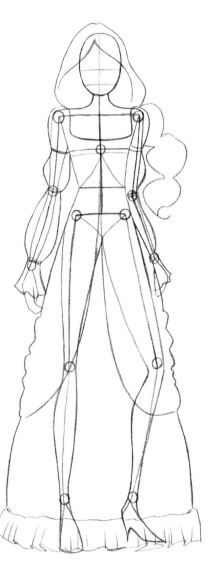

4

Tighten up your sketch, and erase unnecessary pencil marks.

5

Now add youthful lips, heavy lashes, a braid through the hair, and a beaded hairpiece. Then add the dress details, including gathers, folds, and ruffles, as well as flowing sleeves. Use soft, curved vertical lines to convey the feel of the gathered material. Add a brooch and some beaded detail at the bust.

6

Layer in the large areas of color using markers; then shade the folds and gathers with slightly darker-toned colored pencils. Add multi-tonal golden hair and red rubies in the hairpiece and brooch for the finishing touches.

When designing costumes, you might find it helpful to watch old movies or consult historical references to ensure that your sketches are accurate for the time period.

Blushing Bride

For a bride, the wedding day is all about the dress. Custom wedding-gown designers have the opportunity to create something uniquely special for each bride—and no two dresses are usually exactly alike. But bridal designers aren't limited to wedding dresses. They also design gowns for the maid of honor, the bridesmaids and flower girls, and the mothers of the bride and groom.

1

Start with a simple stick figure.

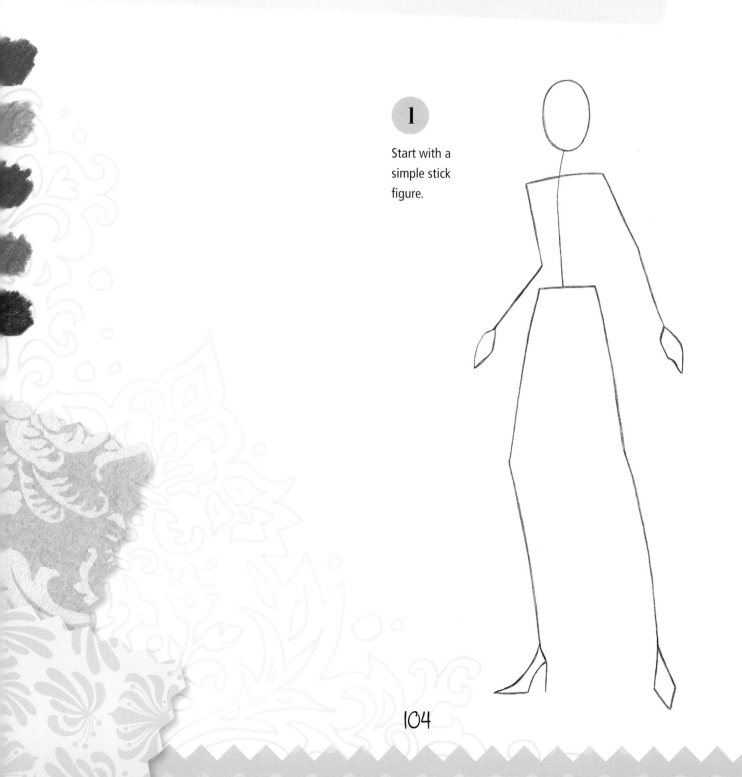

2

Add circles at the joints and gridlines to fill in the volume and form the body. Make sure that the arms and neck look soft and graceful, but don't worry too much about the legs and pelvis—they will be concealed under the gown.

3

Draw a midline and gridlines
on the face to help position
the eye and mouth. Rough in
a sweeping updo with some
gentle curls cascading down.
Draw the outline of a classic,
off-the-shoulder gown with a
fitted bodice and full ball skirt
at the natural waist. Add a faint
outline of the veil to indicate
the light, airy texture of the
tulle.

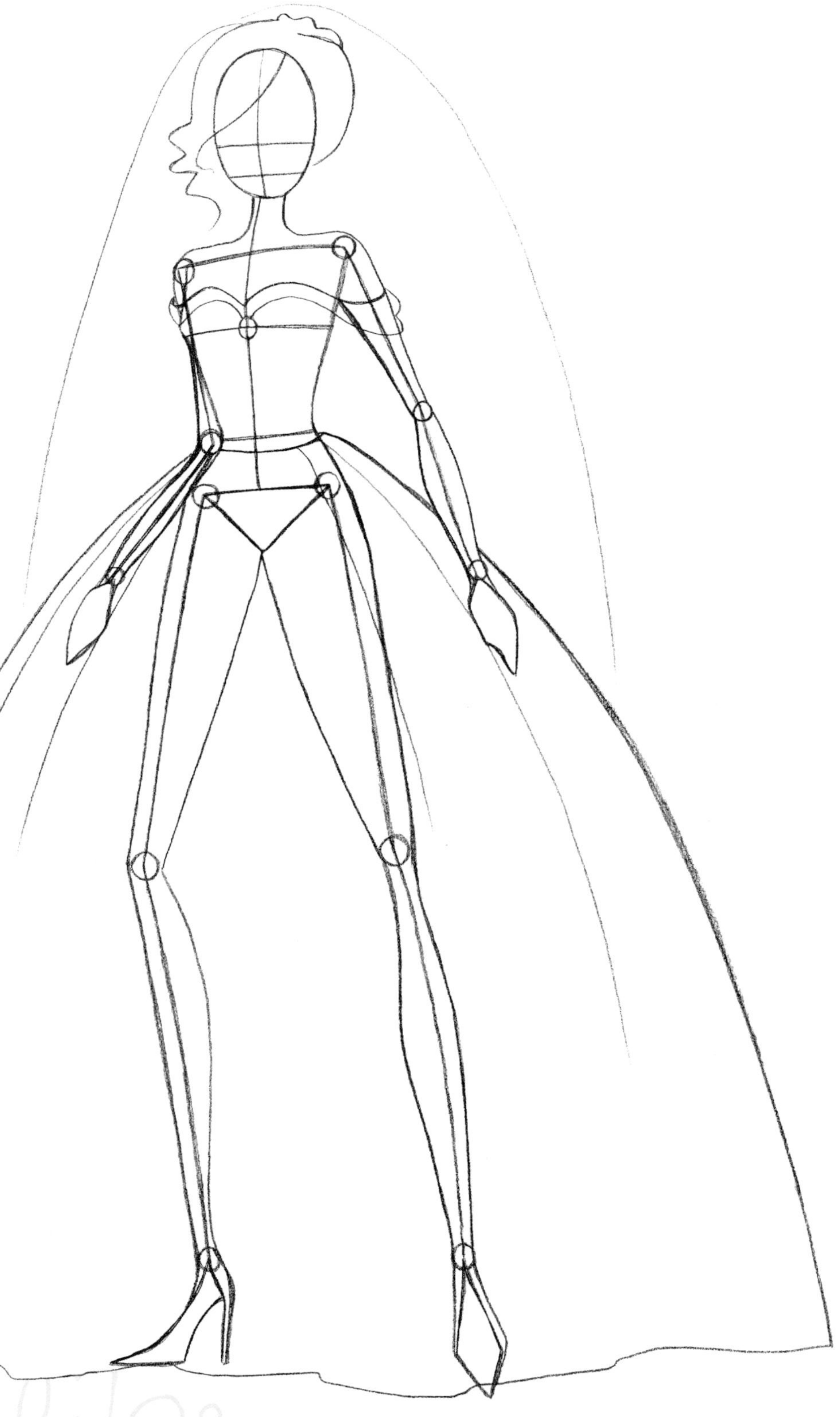

4

Erase unnecessary lines,
including the legs under
the dress.

5

Now add the details, including two pleats on each side of the skirt front, princess seams, and intricate lace appliqués on the skirt hem and bodice. Accessories include dangly beaded earrings, an antique hairpiece, white gloves with covered buttons, and, of course, the delicate veil.

6

Bridal gowns need very little coloring since they are white, but strategically placed shading in cool blues and lavenders convey white better than no color at all. The trick is to use a light hand and only apply the color in areas of detail and shadow. A few wisps of color in the veil work the same magic. Add warm skin tones and rich hair color using a few shades of marker and pencil. Finish with a bit of pink shading on the cheeks to indicate a true "blushing" bride.

Chapter 6

Fashion Figure Templates

Trace or photocopy
these templates as often
as you wish to practice
your technique and
to create an endless
number of fashion
designs.

113

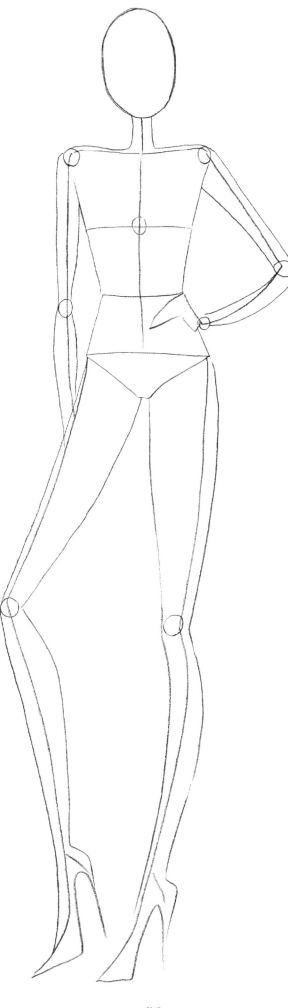

115

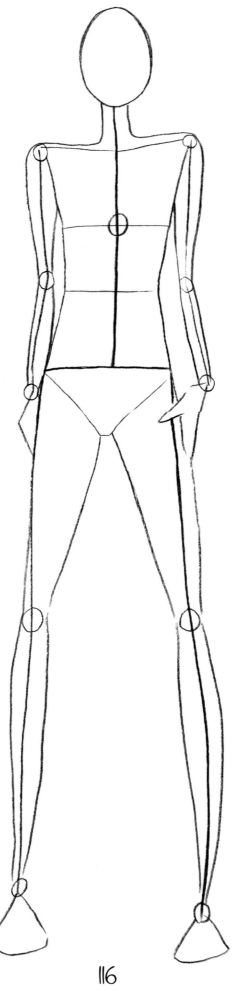

116

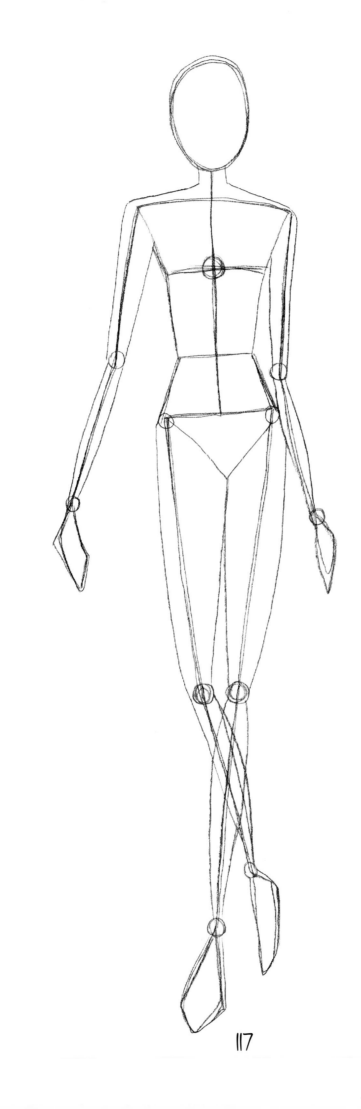

117

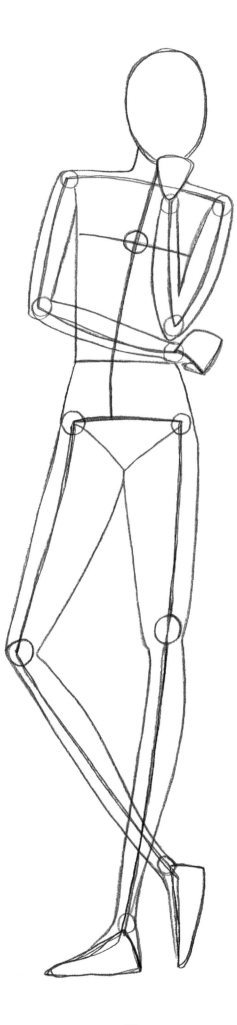

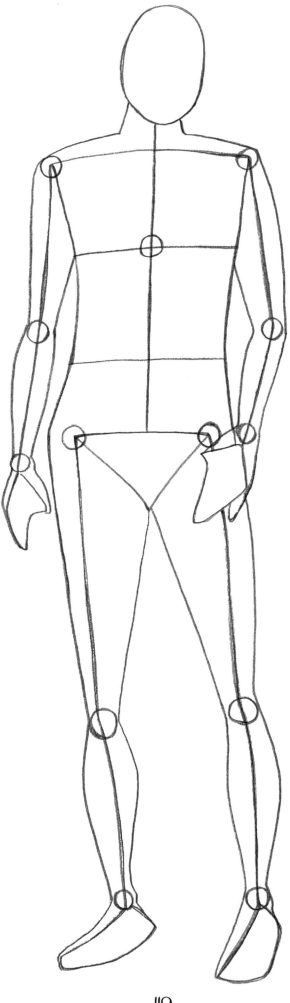

119

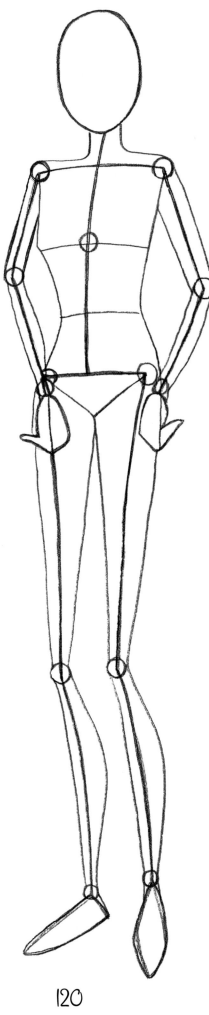

120

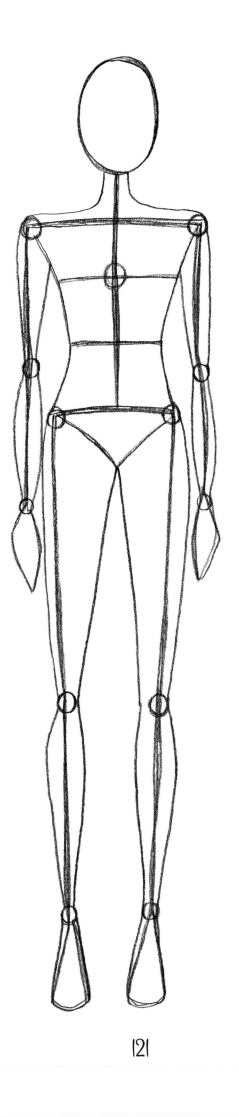

122

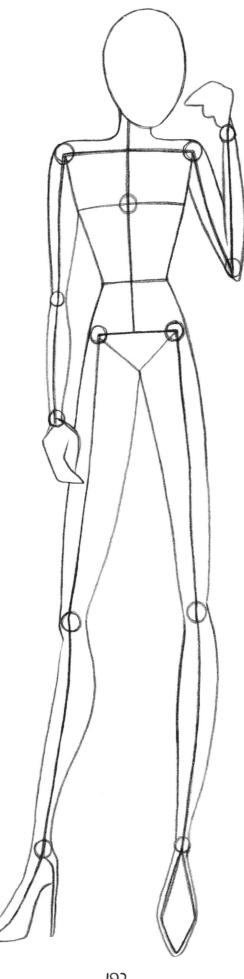

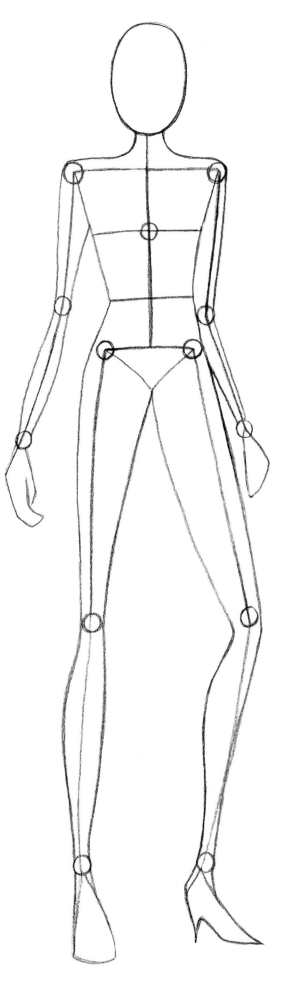

124

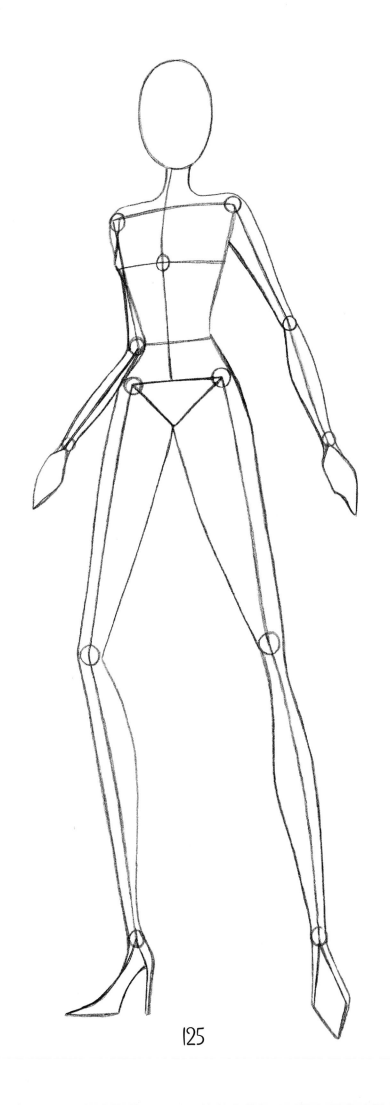

125

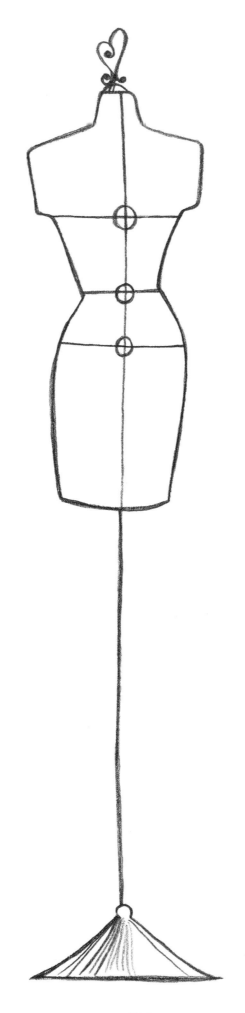

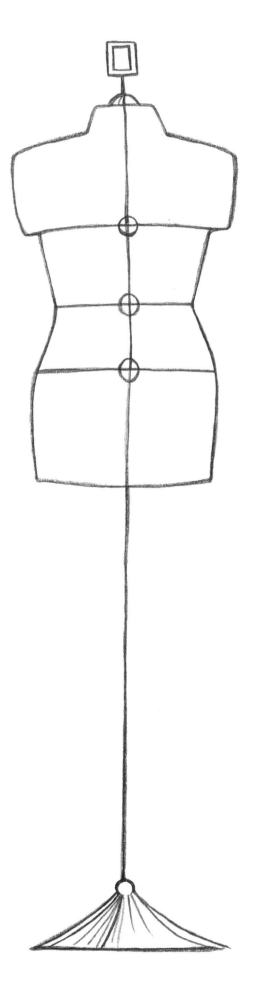

127

About the Artist

Stephanie Corfee is a full-time freelance artist and designer living in Malvern, Pennsylvania. She has worked in advertising and marketing and previously owned her own wedding gown design studio. Today Stephanie enjoys the creative freedom that comes from owning her own business while doing what she loves. She has a colorful, bohemian personal aesthetic and loves creating fun, whimsical art for children. Visit www.stephaniecorfee.com.